I0504791

Shock and Awe, Recruit!

How I Learned the Fundamentals of Advertising

in Marine Corps Basic Training

A Transformational Book By: Brett G Jones

Table of Contents

For the Joneses...every last one of us.

Chapter 1: The Five Ps - Not product, price, placement, promotion, and people

Any student of marketing is familiar with the Five Ps: Product, Price, Promotion, Place, and People. I'd like to start this book talking about The Five Ps I learned from a motivated drill instructor: ***Prior Planning Prevents Poor Performance***. In my efforts to prepare a collection of insights for my dear readers, I've done my best to execute the five Ps my drill instructors taught me. I've prepared and planned as best I can to deliver the prime performance, I hope you'll enjoy in these coming pages.

I've reached out to my old drill instructors from 17 years ago to get their perspectives on the times, both my times then and the times now. I've reached out to my mentors of years gone by, from Euro RSCG DSW, to MRM // McCann, Ogilvy, and Madras, and asked for their input on drafts before this first edition is to be published. I've reached out to recruiters, talent managers, and HR executives from around our industry to get their perspectives on Marine Corps veteran employees and their performance in our crazy world of advertising. I've even reached out to employers outside our industry to see how veterans get along. Lastly, I've submitted a draft for pre-publication review to make sure the Department of Defense is good with my perspective. They may not agree with my perspective on everything, but at least they know I respect the traditions. You're not about to read a slanderous recounting of my time in basic training. I didn't have a bad time. I had a great time.

My preparations have been in the hopes that you, dear reader, will be emboldened to strike out in a rewarding career in marketing or advertising--creative fields full of a bunch of misplaced misfits like yourself. While this book is meant primarily for Marine Corps veterans (because you are my brothers and sisters) this book might also pass muster with all veterans, and shucks, maybe even the regular civilians looking to get into marketing or advertising. Because I believe two things: 1) leadership is for everyone; not just Marines, and 2) a life lived in (and adjacent to) creativity is a life not wasted. I want to bring more Marines to the Creatives and more Creatives to the Marines. Leadership will help our industry's creativity and creativity will give Marines and other veterans an outlet to express their own perspectives...and get paid.

I have done my prior planning to prevent poor performance. I hope it pays its due reward and I find many more Marines and other motivated, dedicated, hard-chargers in this industry by the time my career comes to an end. If you do find your way into the industry, Marine or otherwise, please drop me a line on the social sphere. I'd love to hear about it, so hit me on my Twitter handle @bgjones

Before I go on and talk about my glorified war stories of basic training (and that's all I'll talk about here, because my time in the fleet ended up being pretty rosy in Okinawa and San Diego, so don't go thinking I'm some kind of war hero), I'd like to mention that the insights I lay out here are only insights. That's it. I'm not claiming authority outside of anything but my own subjective opinion. My insights and mine alone. These insights have not been approved or endorsed by the United States Marine Corps or the Department of Defense. Nor are these insights endorsed by any of the esteemed and aforementioned organizations of the trade, like McCann and Ogilvy. These insights are merely derived from my perceptions and I'm sharing in the hopes that you, dear reader, may come to understand as my one-point perspective. A one-point perspective that may not work for anyone other than me.

However (comma, with a slight pause for effect), I do hope that my perspective is something that might be valued. As I, for one, have longed for, and still long for a voice to guide me through the chaos. I don't think my voice is *the* voice for everyone, but it might be just right for that one devil dog with a dream like me and doesn't mind the tones or sounds of my voice. Even if just one motivator puts down this book or hears one of my podcasts, and goes on to a rewarding career in marketing or advertising, I'll be a happy motivator myself. If I can be that voice for even just one motivated individual, then it'll be all worth it. This passenger will be happy as an astronaut on launch day.

Prior planning is something to be done before striking out on any endeavor. Prior to entering basic training in the spring of 2002, I spent time in the Delayed Enlistment Program. During that time from early December to early April, me and the other poolees would muster for physical training and study. At the time, one needed 3 pull ups, a decent mile, a handful of sit-ups, and half a brain to get into Marine Corps basic training. I'll admit, I've never been the best at pull-ups, but I've always been a natural runner. Even if a poolee had met the minimum threshold, you really can't be too prepared. Our recruiters encouraged constant training. Even before basic training, these seasoned Marines had lessons to give us. To prepare us for the months to come.

In those months before basic training, I must have watched Full Metal Jacket at that recruiter's office 117 times. It was on repeat, nearly every day, like clockwork. The morning show and the afternoon show. The recruiters would let us poolees hang out at the office, so long as we were 'watching Full Metal Jacket' we were getting relevant training. Even though I came from a great family and should have been spending time with them, I spent a lot of time at the recruiter's office. A few of us poolees didn't come from backgrounds as sheltered and privileged as my own, so I got to know a few kids that came from hard backgrounds. Kids from 'the other side of the tracks,' already scarred by emotional or physical trauma. I knew they'd make it through basic training, because you could see the hardness in their eyes and hear it in their voice. Would I?

The only way to find out is to keep moving forward. I kept training. Studied for their placement test and passed without a problem. My recruiter told me I was 'too smart to be bullet fodder' so he asked me if I liked jets or helicopters. Of course, I do. He asked if I would like to work on them. Of course, I would. Great, he said, we'll get you a job in the Air Wing, 6000 field. Sign here. It turns out I ended up as a glorified car mechanic. I worked on the diesel tugs that pulled the aircraft around. Landed the MOS of 6072. Ground Support Equipment. There is a lesson to be learned here about prior planning.

The Marine Corps has a phrase, "per the needs." As in, "you are being reassigned to Bahrain," a place most Americans couldn't point to on a map, and a station where no Marine ever really wants to go. There is a strategic mission requiring your presence for one year, maybe more, and you will accept this mission, *per the needs* of the Marine Corps." This is a lesson I learned about being assigned a military occupational specialty. Everyone gives recruiters a hard time. I ended up loving my job, the people I met, and places I saw. I got lucky, so what if I'm not working on planes or helicopters. I'm on the flight line. I'm in the game. I'm a United States Marine and I'm in this game for life now. Once and always, as they say. It's true. I can't get over it, so I've gotta get it outta me. That's why you're spending time with this book, dear reader.

Maybe in advertising, you'll land a job you don't feel is the right fit. Figure it out. Do that job and do it as best you damn can until the job is done and do it over again for two years. One year isn't enough to learn it and three is too long to stay anywhere unless you find out you love it. It two years, you'll find out if you love it or not. Give the job the time to prove to why the needs of advertising may just bring you what you're looking for. Nobody else's perspective of what it's like to work in this industry will be able to give you your perspective of this industry. Not even I, Brett G Jones, with all my *savoir faire* may give it to you. Just like Marine Corp Basic Training or The Matrix...

...you'll just have to go and find out for yourself.

In today's gig economy, and the pace of change in technology, you no longer need a four-year degree to join big and exciting companies. Apple, Google, and others have removed the requirement. That means a whole host of young people may enlist in this crazy creative field. If you really want to join our ranks, please, please, do your prior planning. Prevent poor performance by deciding if you really want that four-year degree. You might not need it if you've got the chops. It just takes confidence and a little desktop research to walk into an interview and crush it. Nothing beats on the job training.

If you do want to go to, or finish school, find yourself a good school with a good creative program like Brigham Young University or University of Virginia. Even Georgia State has a great Creative Writing department. This industry is full of misplaced misfits and the more you can surround yourself with creative types, the better. If you already do, that's great. Go find even crazier creatives. This industry attracts creative types like sailors to strip joints.

Whether you're courting a lady of the evening or a job offer, commit to endless commitment to planning and preparation. Even after you get a job, you'll have to learn, unlearn, and relearn for the rest of your natural life, so says the futurist and Alvin Toffler. This is an industry full of transformation, so adaptation is key and it's easiest when you plan for it. Toffler also likes to say, "If you don't have a strategy, then you're part of someone else's strategy.'

Chapter 2: Take it Chow to Chow – breaking up your time into manageable increments

I learned a lot of incredibly valuable things in Marine Corps Basic Training, from military history, to martial arts, marksmanship, and how to bounce a quarter off a tight rack (that's a bed for you civilians out there). One thing I learned that proved to be one of the most valuable things, if not the most valuable thing is this: no matter the torture or torment, the drill instructors have to feed you three meals a day and they have to put you to sleep at some point. Even during The Crucible, we got like an hour or two of sleep each night. Those moments alone in your sleeping bag are some of the most glorious moments of basic. No drill instructor yelling at you, no recruit mucking up the operational efficiency of your fire team's performance, no responsibility but to rest, recharge, and reflect on all the power moves you made that day.

Taking it chow to chow is all about time management. In advertising, for almost every team, every day is different. There are new challenges to face, new pitches to win, new problems to solve, new arguments to settle, new egos to tend to, new people to train, and certainly not least the clients. Those clients will keep you on your toes with their relentless leaning on the agency for more work with less money in less time...oh, and they want it better than last time. It gets overwhelming.

What's a warrior to do? Break up the day. Break each challenge up into manageable tasks and take those tasks on one by one until it's chow time. Recharge the batteries with some chow and some chat and then get back after it until the challenge is done.

Break the day up into manageable increments from the moment you wake up. Every morning at basic, the first thing we did was make the bed. William McRaven, a US Navy Admiral, wrote a book called, 'Make Your Bed.' He says, "If you want to change the world, start off by making your bed." It is the first task of the day and if you do that successfully, it will inspire you to do the next task, and the next one. He says if you can't do the little things right, you'll never get the big things right. And if, by chance, you have a tough day, at the end of it, you get to come home to a bed you made...and rest until the next day to take the challenges head on with your warrior spirit.

These seemingly impossible challenges of the day become more manageable when you break them up into moments. Each task has a beginning, a middle, and an end, just like every good story. The hardest part is often the motivation to start the task, so just make the damn bed and start your day. When you know that no task will ever overtake those moments you have to yourself in the morning, at meal times, and in the evening, and you use those moments to rest, recharge, reflect, and dare I say be grateful for the challenges of the day, then no task will ever seem unmanageable, because you know it will get done with enough time and effort. In between now and when the task gets done, hopefully you have some nice dreams, some nice meals, and some nice conversations with friends and co-workers along the way. (In basic, they wouldn't let us talk at meal time, so take advantage of those moments and get to know your people.) After enough meals and enough shut eye, that big tasks will be done and you'll be on to the next one.

This whole notion of taking the struggle from chow to chow relies heavily upon your ability to remain in the now moments. If you are unable to be present in those moments and you keep thinking about work when you're falling asleep or working while you're eating, then you're gonna burn out. The key is to be present and focused on you during those moments and put the work aside.

It's too easy to skip a meal or bring your lunch back to your desk instead of going out to lunch with a co-worker or by yourself. If you do bring a co-worker, don't talk about the work, talk about the weather or the latest book you're reading. If you're stuck in the slog all day, all long, then there will be nothing interesting about you in 5 years, you'll just be a working stiff. No culture, no real friends, no self-worth beyond your work. That's not what life is about. Life is about those moments in between the work. Life is about enjoying our time here and the art we get to create together as humans being human beings, that's where the art comes from.

Find your strength in the now moments and the failures of the past or the trials of the future no longer seem as daunting. Renew your strength when you wake and when you fall asleep by reminding yourself of all you've accomplished throughout the day. Revive your strength throughout the day with a good meal and some time away from the struggles of the day. Your strength comes from within. Nobody can give it to you. You'll find your strength in those moments in between the battles of the day. When you find it and you discover how easy it is to tackle anything with this chow to chow mindset, then you'll be able to take on any brief, any deadline, any challenge the clients present you or your team. Once I realized after a few weeks of basic that this inner strength is all I need to endure any torment or torture, I found peace.

With my inner strength the rest of basic training became an easy game.

You don't need basic training of any variety to find your inner strength. You may find it over the course of any adversity. Any agency has shared hardships and hard work. The dangers may not be mortal but they are sometimes insufferable. These trials strengthen an agency and reduces problems in the long run, when the agency is trained to handle them. Sharing adversity will develop teamwork, improve morale, and create a feeling of unbounded loyalty. The foundation for retention. When the adversity is met by motivation and teamwork, the agency will brag about their tough clients, because they can handle it...and get paid handsomely to do so.

A couple years after basic training, I was voluntold for a three-week intensive course to become a Marine Corps Martial Arts instructor. Because of this inner strength I joined a class of 12 and came out as one of 4 graduates. Our lead instructor, Staff Sergeant Brown, taught me the phrase, "Adversity is when one is introduced to oneself." Some credit it to Einstein. Staff Sergeant Brown attributed the phrase to some Spartan warrior from days long gone by, if I recall. I credit it to an unknown Jones from an adjacent cosmos giving her wisdom from a more enlightened society.

In advertising there is plenty of adversity with all these demands and deadlines we put ourselves through. Sometimes we play the hurry up and wait game and all of the sudden we have plenty of time for chow. One of the things I love most is a spontaneous funch on a Tuesday.

The *funch* is a fun lunch, longer than an hour, but not by much (per the needs) and at a restaurant that's a sit-down place. Order a drink first and order one for those that do, don't ask them if they want one, ask them if they'd like to join you. Who turns down an invitation for a rosé at 12:15 pm on a hot Tuesday? When your team knows that on any given day, you'll make sure their calendar is clear for a funch, you're gonna get performance out of that team the next time they face adversity. That seafood tower or Korean BBQ and a few laughs will go a long way for your copywriter that has to churn out 5,000 words in 1 hour on a topic so dry it makes the cotton mouth of a middle-school motivator seem moist.

In closing, take every day from chow to chow, dear motivators. It's not a bad way to go through any adversity, or for that matter, any kind of life.

Chapter 3: Your Body as a Robot – The body will go longer than the mind ever will, so train your mind

A body needs food. A robot needs energy. Food is energy. The body is a robot. The mind is the operating system. The heart is where the user ports in to operate. Some hearts are born warriors, some have to find it in themselves through life's adversity.

This one I may not have learned in basic training. My understanding of the mind body relationship likely came from conversations with a dear friend I met in my Intro to Philosophy class at the Salt Lake Community College in Utah. We'll call him Jerome. I dropped out of high school to go to college and in this class, I asked some questions of my professor, Dr. Wright. Some of those questions made Jerome laugh, and he likely thought of me as a bit of an oddity, not unlike himself. We began our friendship over chimichangas and burritos at Alberto's and he would tell me about his band. As an impressionable 17-year-old and aspiring guitarist, I was all-in. After we got to know each other well enough, he invited me over to his house. At that house we'd rip cannabis and talk about our philosophy class or rock music.

One day, as was my tradition at the time, I dropped by and Jerome was in the basement. As usual, he was deep into a ProTools track, fiddling around. While I was waiting for him to move whatever snare drum snap to the right position behind the bass lick, he threw an audio engineering magazine at me and said there was an interesting article in the pub about the body as a robot. The author spun a yarn about how there are certain monotonous tasks that might feel tedious or too repetitive to one's liking. When one must commit to those tasks, one might consider operating the body as a robot. Let the robot do the work while the mind did something more enjoyable, like drinking an iced cocktail at the beach with fresh flowers for your lady delivered by another robot...I mean flower gal. We're all robots, really, if you think about it long enough.

The robot has functions and those functions are performed dutifully and masterfully. Now our drill instructors did not literally break each one of us down psychologically to become 'mindless robot drones,' as some in the First Civilian Division might suspect. The warriors they make in basic training are individuals. They have personalities and character just like everybody else. We are not all the same and I believe that many Americans know a great many veterans and their perception of us, if you ask them, is that we represent the great cross-section of America. We come from everywhere. Every state (and a whole lot from Texas) sees their sons and daughters voluntarily step forward.

That might be what makes us special, that gumption. That's why we volunteer our robots for the job. I guess my gumption comes from reading a lot of science-fiction at a young age that lead to a never-ending fascination with the great mysteries of life. With all the science fiction and self-examination that Socrates told me to do, it was the adversity I faced in basic training that drove me fully into the realization that the body is a robot. How did I do it? I made cottage cheese my robot's batteries.

My uncle told me when he went through basic training (Vietnam era) that the secret to chow is cottage cheese. It's high in protein and you can eat a helluva-lot-of-it in five minutes.

The whole trick with bootcamp, my uncle told me, is to remember that it's all a game. The game is about the drill instructors breaking your body down and building it into a machine. A warfighting and killing machine. There are drill instructors for different types of knowledge. Drill knowledge. History and military knowledge. Physical fitness knowledge. The Senior Drill Instructor is there to keep them all in line. You don't ever rat to the Senior, but know that if he sees you giving everything you have and he sees the drill instructors breaking you too hard, he'll call them off. They follow orders. His job is to make sure every recruit is prepared for combat after about 90 days. If you see a recruit you've been helping wash out because they don't have the physicality, athleticism, mentality, or health to make it. Don't let it get you down. You've gotta keep moving forward. The name of the game is to make it through each day...day in and day out...for 90 days, and then you're a Marine, but until then, you'll always be their recruit. They will do everything they can to make you not want to be a Marine. They don't want any soul that does not have what it takes to be a warrior to wear that Eagle, Globe, and Anchor. They will run you. They will push you. They will take the strongest among you and break you.

As a recruit, your identity does break down, but it never completely dies. Nothing ever dies. It transforms. Once each recruit finds that inner strength they need to survive, once they discover their *mind* will break before their **body** ever does, once a recruit realizes they have what it takes to make it through whatever adversity is presented before them, then they realize in their hearts they are already a *warrior*. The Eagle, Globe, and Anchor will only make their mind and their robot a Marine.

In every one of our hearts, we have what it takes to be a warrior. Basic training only makes Marines, it's the *polycosmic happening* that makes a warrior.

A good warrior loves his robot.

This is my robot...

*This is my robot. There are many like it but this one is mine. My robot is my
best friend. It is my life. I must master it as I master my life. Without
me, my robot is useless. Without my robot, I am useless. I must use
my robot true. I must be more effective than my enemy who is trying
to kill me. I must love them and their robots before they hate me and
mine. I will...*

*My robot and I know that what counts in life is not the words we say, the
noise of our voice, nor the smoke we make. We know that it's the love
that counts. We will love...*

*My robot is human, even as I, because it is my life. Thus, I will learn it as a
brother. I will learn its weaknesses, its strength, its parts, its
accessories, its sights and its potential. I will keep my body clean and
ready, even as I am clean and ready. We are a part of each other.*

*Before God, I swear this creed. My robot and I are the defenders of
creativity. We are the masters of our enemy. We are the saviors of
my life.*

So be it, until victory is all humanity and there is no enemy, but peace!

I've adapted the rifleman's creed to fit my robot analogy and gave it
the Jones touch of love. For those motivators in the First Civilian
Division, and for the brothers and sisters in the other four branches of
the service that don't come out of basic training with the phrase, *every
Marine a rifleman,* ingrained in your soul, and for those who haven't
seen Stanley Kubrick's, "Full Metal Jacket," you may find the
original text of the Rifleman's Creed, as follows:

This is my rifle. There are many like it, but this one is mine.

My rifle is my best friend. It is my life. I must master it as I must master my life.

Without me, my rifle is useless. Without my rifle, I am useless. I must fire my rifle true. I must shoot straighter than my enemy who is trying to kill me. I must shoot him before he shoots me. I will ...

My rifle and I know that what counts in war is not the rounds we fire, the noise of our burst, nor the smoke we make. We know that it is the hits that count. We will hit ...

My rifle is human, even as I, because it is my life. Thus, I will learn it as a brother. I will learn its weaknesses, its strength, its parts, its accessories, its sights and its barrel. I will keep my rifle clean and ready, even as I am clean and ready. We will become part of each other. We will ...

Before God, I swear this creed. My rifle and I are the defenders of my country. We are the masters of our enemy. We are the saviors of my life.

So be it, until victory is America's and there is no enemy, but peace!

Perhaps it was while I was doing pushups in the surf of the Pacific Ocean when I found my inner strength by thinking about robots and cottage cheese. After that, I loved basic training. Throw a grenade? Rad. Obstacle course? Motivate. Military studies. Who doesn't love a Spartan? Athenians, maybe? Don't get me started with the French. Drill? Give me a rifle, I'll choke Jodi on that parade deck until the cows come home and you stand up and slap your grandma.

Now, before you civilians from the First Civilian Division start Googling 'choking Jodi,' I'll save you a run in with videos you don't want to see...choking Jodi is what the drill instructors tell you to imagine your girlfriend or boyfriend at home, imagine them in all their loveliness, and then imagine them with a lover named, Jodi. Jodi has been there for her needs while her true love is gone. Jodi is beginning to fall for your love and your love is beginning to fall for Jodi, too. What do you want to do? You want to CHOKE JODI with your LEFT HAND. Now what can we visualize with our warrior minds to practice CHOKING JODI?

"THE FORWARD GRIP OF YOUR M-16 WHEN I CALL, 'PORT ARMS' RECRUIT, THAT'S WHAT!!!"

Our drill instructor walked us through this visualization trick in order to create the loudest POP he could get out of our movements when our left hands came across the body to grasp the forward grip of our rifle. The left hand is often the weaker of the two hands when it comes to the input of recruits. Creative minds are often known to be left-handed and some view the military as a place that stifles creativity. I'd offer that it breeds creativity, but who's asking?

In any case, I'm right-handed with a creative mind, so my left hand needed a little creative visualization in order to make it really hit that grip with a real pop. I don't blame the drill instructors for using hate to motivate. It's a powerful tool, hate. Once we all got good at it, though, and we all heard that *POP* in synch for the first time, for me that hate transformed into love. I loved that audible *POP* better than the lover I lost to that mother trucker, Jodi. That love became the motivating factor that fueled my passion for excellence in drill.

Whether you're in basic training trying to figure out how to pull your fellow recruit through a hole in a wall, and that recruit has been deemed, 'lifeless' by your drill instructor; or, you're in a boardroom trying to figure out how to convince a client to work with your agency after an evening drinking with them and their robot being deemed 'lifeless' by alcohol poisoning the night before, you've gotta train your robot to make it through those tough times and train your mind to understand that in the end, it's all just a damn game.

Win. Win at everything you do. Win at push-ups. Win at pull ups. Win at running. Win at fighting. Win your contact report. Win your copy. Win your art. Win your proofreading. Win your pre-pro meeting. Win at numbers. Win at data. Just go out there and win the game. Wake up, eat your Wheaties®, and win. Even when you're failing, you're learning how to win next time, so you're still winning. Winners don't lose, they learn. Winners win by showing up. That's it. Unless you're the French. The French suck. What do they say about those truffle-huffing surrender-monkeys? Their war cry is 'RETREAT!'

I only kid, I love the French, too. It was Stephen Colbert's monologue on the French in an episode of *The Colbert Report* that persuaded me to shake the hatred for the French that my drill instructors instilled in me. I'm lucky that happened, too, because Olivier Duong, a creative partner in business whom I met at Madras Global, happens to be a Vietnamese-French-American fella. In any case, no matter where you got your robot, if you're a motivator, then you're good in my book.

What's a motivator, you ask? A motivator is a motivated, dedicated, hard-charging individual that shows up ready to win...even if they're French. Above all else, dear motivator, remember, your body is a robot so, train your mind. Then you'll have a long and rewarding career in advertising with a bunch of other creative robots with motivating operating systems and their warrior hearts in the world.

Chapter 4: One Mind, Any Weapon – An effective mind will see opportunities everywhere

An effective mind will see opportunities everywhere. This is the one element of the Marine Corps Martial Arts Program that is the dark horse for any Jarhead who wants to impress Corporate America. Marines have a reputation for being dumb, order-taking bullet fodder, that's why they call us Jarheads, because we 'don't have anything between the ears.'

In my era, the Marine Corps Martial Arts Program is the hand-to-hand combat training course for recruits and active duty Marines. No matter how long you've been in my beloved corps, a recruit or Marine *must* test for their Tan Belt. Now, it's been over a decade since I was in, so unless there are some operators out there in deep counterintelligence units practicing some real warfighting instead of training for their belts, I'd wager that *every* Marine must have their Tan Belt by now. If not, you're likely being hunted down by one of my fellow instructors or our instructor trainers, like Staff Sergeant Brown.

The phrase, 'One Mind, Any Weapon' is the veritable slogan of MCMAP. Marine Corps Recruiting Command will tell you it means Marines are armed with "*a combat mindset* and the ability to assess and to act." I'd tell you that in means that motivators in advertising who adopt this mindset are armed with a *brand building mindset* and the ability to assess and act.

Keep your robot as physically fit as you are able and keep your heart as morally straight as possible so you'll be in a position to do the right thing when the time comes. That goes for the robots on the battlefield and the robots in advertising. Whether you're slinging bullets or ads, you've gotta stay tuned. Luck is when preparation meets opportunity. Make your own luck and be a good robot scout. Be prepared. Don't get lazy with the robot. Read Neal Stephenson's essay, 'Arsebestos' and get yourself a treadmill desk so you can respond to your client emails while strolling a leisurely 1.5 miles an hour.

To get an idea of their ethos, I quote Marine Corps Order 1500.54A, establishing the program in 2002, "MCMAP is a synergy of mental, character, and physical disciplines with application across the full spectrum of violence."

Marines focus first on the spirit and the heart. They strive to create a warrior guided by ethics and morals. I strive to lead teams driven by the same ethics and morals. We help each other. We do the right thing when no one is looking. We seek out those in need of defense and defend them. We find those who are harming others and we stop them.

One night after a long day at work, some coworkers whom I saw adversity with on the Cabela's account. We were tasked with building their retail commercial engine from the ground up, we were out drinking our pain away and having a few laughs. As is tradition we ended up at a late-night diner, Veselka. This place is legendary for its perogies (ask for Peoter if you're there late one night and tell them I sent you, he'll remember this story). Just after we sat down, we heard some commotion burst through the front door from 2nd Avenue in the East Village.

Now maybe it had something to do with the fact that my girlfriend (and now wife) was there, but I leaped into action and broke up a fight. The fella was getting pummeled hard by his aggressor in the face. He took a couple more hits before I got there, but all it took was a loud booming voice yelling, "YOUR AGGRESSION IS UNCALLED FOR, SIR! YOU HAVE NO REASON TO BE HITTING THIS MAN. STOP AND EXPLAIN YOURSELF OR LEAVE!"

I've jumped to action a couple other times in my life. I made a dude cry at a destination wedding, once. We were at the hotel bar after the lovely couple's engagement party on Kiawah Island. A passerby there on his stag trip with a couple of bros had his eyes on me for a fight. I'm always keen for a fight because it gives me battle joy, but it doesn't mean I'm gonna take the bait from a hater, especially when there are libations involved. These great times we live in should be for celebrating not for fighting! One of our country's founders, John Adams wrote, "I must study politics and war, that our sons may have liberty to study mathematics and philosophy."

Now, I studied my astronomy and philosophy and I know the physics of a fight. I also know from the art of negotiation that the best way to win a fight is to not start the fight. It's an easy game. Don't hit your opponent, just humiliate them tactfully with your words and send them on their way. I made this dude cry in front of his stags and a few of my friends beside me. He cried not because I hit him, but because after he hit me, I immediately said something calmly to him as I looked him in the eyes, "Your action was unprovoked, your aggression is uncalled for, *sir*, and I demand an apology." Then I kept his gaze and waited until he started crying.

I think it was Winston Churchill that said something like, 'Tact is the ability to tell someone to go to hell and enjoy the trip.'

I wouldn't tell you if it weren't true and I'm not telling you because I want to sound macho or mighty, even though I am. I'm telling you because it illustrates the point about a warrior and leader with ethics and morals. The Marine Corps doesn't have a trademark on leadership. They don't own it. Nor do they own ethics or morals. It doesn't take

90 days of basic training to behave like an upstanding citizen. It takes the commitment to yourself in your heart to make yourself a motivator. Take the 11 leadership principles of leadership learned in basic training to the world of advertising with all your gumption and you'll begin to hone the 14 leadership traits in a new way. The mind you've got will be tuned to recognize opportunity everywhere.

Be there for your people and your people will be there for you. Notice them. Exercise your situational awareness and step into action when called for, not when called upon. Understand the commander's intent and execute accordingly. Not all organizations have great leadership in every office. Some regions thrive while others suffer. Everybody wants to work at the hot creative shop. If you're lucky enough to experience the pros like McCann or Ogilvy, then go where the suffering is and stop the bleeding, clear the airways, and start the breathing. Check for wounds after life is revived and dress them. Once the body is better, send the body back into the field and go find another problem to solve. You'll begin to establish a reputation as a leader in your field in no time.

Fix your future now by fortifying your mind with this military mindset in corporate America from the get go. Don't let it go if you've already got it. The Marines are a fraternity with a tradition of excellence in leadership dating back 244 years. Each branch of the military has rich traditions of leadership. Utilize the leadership principles and exercise their traits. Your mind will soon be supported by the best minds in the business because true leadership is hard to come by in this day in age. I think this is because of two fundamental points: 1) people are afraid of being held accountable for failure, and 2) leadership isn't easy (see point 1).

Chapter 5: BAMCIS – The 6 Troop Leading Steps

Being held accountable for failure sucks. It's not fun. Nearly everyone is angry or upset. The client is yelling at you while the phone is on mute. The creative directors are yelling at each other about poor account management. Your account executive looks like a fresh recruit fresh out of processing and is typing notes rapidly on her computer while leaning her head down to the speaker phone to catch the part where the client just asked for the next round by Friday afternoon (and it's Friday morning). It's in those moments one asks oneself, "Why advertising? Why not sell...coffee?"

Those moments come few and far between depending on either the temperament of the day-to-day client (which is often influenced by the lead client); or, the efficacy of the agency leadership, namely the creative directors and/or account directors on the day-to-day business (which is often influenced by the lead business manager, sometimes a creative minded account person or an account minded creative person).

The business manager, meaning the agency's client facing representatives (at Ogilvy we called them Executive Group Directors or Managing Directors) is to help translate business speak into creative speak and creative speak back into business speak, when called for. It isn't always necessary. The EGDs and MDs set the tone for the entire account. How they manage their teams and inspire motivation for peak performance and do their best to keep morale up varies. Like Kanye said at his Sunday Service featured on My Next Guest Needs No Introduction with David Letterman, "there are basically only two buttons to bush in this life and that's either love or fear." Whether you're an EGD running an account team or an ECD (Executive Creative Director) running a creative team, it's your choice about what button to press and when.

In my experience, both in basic training, and in advertising, is that you never find a manager who hits one button all the time, and even if they're hitting the love button, sometimes it feels like fear. This is best illustrated in basic training by one of my Drill Instructors, the Knowledge Hat. I think it wasn't until month two or so that he finally told us what the difference between a 'knife hand' and a 'pointed finger' meant, well...at least to him. It didn't mean jack to me or my fellow recruits until he told us. Now that I'm telling you, maybe you'll pick it up in your management style.

Accountability must be placed upon somebody when failure is happening. Most often, one will defer blame to authority. That authority must take action to correct that mentality by illustrating the history of events leading to failure and logically explain what went wrong so the breakdown doesn't happen again. Recruits will stammer out explanations about how they couldn't get the particular task completed properly, and the drill instructor would yell at the recruit. Drill instructors yell. It doesn't mean they're angry. They just want to make a learning experience out of almost every waking moment, so they yell at one recruit so that all the other recruits may witness the lesson. If the drill instructor knew the fault is entirely on the recruit, while he yelled, he would use a 'knife hand,' or the hand with five extended fingers, like a karate chop. This hand would be thrust through the air toward the recruit at such alarming speeds, the other recruits nearby sometimes flinch for fear of the recruit being knocked into them by the drill instructors flailing phalanges.

The 'knife hand' is a signal that the fault is entirely upon the recruit, because the recruit had everything required to complete the task. He just couldn't get it because he was either: too nervous, too slow, or too dense to understand simple instructions. If there was something that the drill instructor realized he forgot to include in the task, like a particular set of instructions, or the packet of materials prepared was missing something because they, too, are running on little to no sleep, he would merely point a finger, instead of using the fearful knife hand. He would yell, but then explain that the recruit didn't notice soon enough the missing materials, or lack of instruction, and that they should have spoken up sooner, because in a foxhole, your buddy next to you just died from your lack of preparation.

The one finger places some blame upon the recruit, but the other fingers are pointing back at the drill instructor. The leader will always take accountability, when called for. After bootcamp, when every moment is no longer a lesson, and a recruit becomes Marine, the lessons are best reserved for private conversations.

Chastise in private, praise in public is a good motto to remember. Rarely would you see a recruit dragged away for a real ear bender, but in the fleet, I saw it all the time. Public shame is no good for morale in the fleet. It makes people feel...sticky. Same goes for the world advertising. Don't dehumanize anybody, ever, if you can help it, least of all, in front of other people. And when you're in private with your small teams or team member and having tough conversations, don't point the finger when you should be using a knife hand...and vice versa.

It's important to remember this as any type of manager in the advertising business, so that when you execute BAMCIS, you may help keep your troops in line with the mission and its objectives. Let's quickly look at the acronym that has helped to bring about so many superior victories against incredible odds and add a little bit of advertising lingo for context:

BAMCIS - The 6 Troop Leading Steps for Executives

1. **B**egin the planning - Brief project - input brief - develop scope (command)

2. **A**rrange for reconnaissance - Begin strategy - brief and resource (plan)

3. **M**ake the reconnaissance - Execute strategy - development (strategize)

4. **C**omplete the plan - Develop creative - reviews and approvals (create)

5. **I**ssue the order - Deploy assets - go-to-market deployment (support)

6. **S**upervise - Retain and optimize - consult as required for optimization (report)

The system is simple. Before you can do anything, you've gotta make a plan. A lot of time in advertising is wasted waiting for the client and the lead account manager trying to figure out what the plan is. Whether the lead client is incompetent, the lead account manager is incompetent, or any other myriad of reasons on either side's chain of command, figuring out what the plan is the hardest part to starting any project. If you don't at least try and figure it out, it'll cost a lot more, last a lot longer, and create a helluva lot more headaches than anyone wants to deal with. You won't have headaches if you'll follow BAMCIS, so let's break them down one by one.

The first of the 6 Basic Troop Leading Steps is to **Begin the Planning**. That means the lead account manager either takes an input brief from the client, as is tradition; or, a proactive agency will encourage the lead account manager to pull briefs from their teams to take to the clients for approval. The latter often will command more respect for the agency partners, so long as the ideas are good. Good ideas come from anywhere in the team, not just the creative department. That's the value of a great agency, the whole shop is usually creatively minded. From the finance gal to the print production manager, we all have our passions and quirks, even if we don't roll up our skinny jeans and wear curled mustaches. Before a client can get those ideas out of the agency they've just briefed, they've gotta pay one way or the other. Either by awarding the multi-million-dollar business to the lead agency in a new business pitch, or by agreeing to pay a project fee, as negotiated by the account lead.

After the client agrees to a brief, the lead account manager will formalize a scope for signatures. Without breaking down the bureaucratic solutions to that process I've experienced, it's a relatively simple engagement. Two parties agree to a document that ties a monetary value to the product or services provided. In this case, ads for money. Ads nowadays come in all different shapes and sizes. What goes into the ads and the ideas behind them can get pricey. Before your client ever loads them into their distribution channels a team asks themselves a ton of questions. Where will the logo go and how big should it be? Wait, we need a call to action, what are we selling? Who knows the name of the product? What are the competitors and what are they saying about their product? What agency works for the competitors and how do they think? What about our consumers, what are they saying about our client's product? What's the price? Should we list the price to make it seem more valuable? Should we offer a discount or is that cheap? Do we want long form copy or just a big headline?

A lot of those questions are to be answered in step two and three of the 6 Basic Troop Leading Steps. **Arrange for Reconnaissance** and **Make the Reconnaissance**. Recon is just a military word for research. Do your research. If you have a planner slash strategist at the ready, use them. They'll help make your tight input brief into a tight creative brief if you're on the account side. If you find yourself on the creative side, then study the brief and then go do more research. Clients love the agencies that bring fresh points-of-view. A fresh perspective is the only reason people will listen to anybody these days. Once you start spouting the same old same old, you lose the audience. Agencies know their client's brands and sometimes even their businesses better than their clients do. That's the value of a great agency. Those agencies recognize great talent. Great talent knows leadership. Do your research. Plan for and make the reconnaissance like your life and career depend on it. Teach your mind what it needs to know for your heart to recognize the great work and your robot will win.

The fourth of the 6 Basic Troop Leading Steps is to **Complete the Plan**. This can take a while in advertising. Once the reconnaissance is finished, the internal brief to the creative team may finally be conducted. Think about that for a minute, the client came to a creative agency for a creative product and there were three steps before the first creative order is given. That's how an agency maintains profitability. If agencies skipped over the first three steps and briefed a creative team without agreements as who, what, when, or why they want to say what they want to say, how much time would be wasted by absolutely everybody involved? A good account leader will ask the tough questions up front, make sure the clients do their job first, before they go spin the resources of the rest of the agency. That's what makes an agency a great success, time and effort. Ideas are useless if they're shot in the wrong direction.

Complete the Planning in advertising means, the scope has been approved, the brief has been approved, the creative has been approved, the media plan has been approved, all the money is in the right hands and the light is ready to go LIVE. Complete the Plan doesn't mean you're ready to hit GO just yet, that's the client's call. It just means you've got a solid plan. Sometimes, in this business, I'll hear of a multi-million-dollar client will take the agency through a year of work, only to pull the plug because of a failure to listen to the principle outlined in Chapter One of this book. Do you remember it, dear motivator? Our five Ps? Prior Planning Prevents Poor Performance. A Complete Plan has all the elements in place to issue the order that will result in peak performance. That peak performance becomes addicting, really quick. Once you taste peak performance, it's hard to palate anything else.

Step 5 is a crucial step in the 6 Basic Troop Leading Steps, **Issue the Order**. This is when the client green lights and deploys the campaign and the agency waits for a phone call from the client or vendor. If the account lead is good and the team is aligned, the call doesn't come. More often than not, something slips through the cracks. There are a lot of moving parts these days. Take Mountain Dew, for example. Just last week, they released a new line of bottles celebrating each of the 50 states. The art on the bottle had a map of the United States of America and on the map, the Upper Peninsula of Michigan was not painted the same color as Michigan, it looked like it was a part of Wisconsin. To PepsiCo's credit, the Mountain Dew Brand Team and their agency leaped into action. They designed a fresh "Upper Peninsula" logo and handed them out free by the case at the county fair. They took accountability and made a swift and decisive action to make change happen. The results, as they say, are history. This motivator will give a crisp high five to each member of that team, should ever our paths cross. They executed on a principle I'll outline more in my next chapter about Commander's Intent. For now, back to the basics.

The order, when issued, is often coupled with celebrations. Teams will go out for drinks after work on both client and agency sides. Sometimes they'll all go together. It's an exciting time to bring plans to life—to create something from nothing. There may have been some adversity along the way, but we learned about each other and ourselves. We learned how to be better copywriters, better account managers, better developers, or admins. At least I hope the teams I run with do. I make sure to celebrate the wins and encourage learning from losses. There are no real failures, only opportunities to learn for the next round. And there is always another round. First another round of drinks, though...

Once we've dusted off our hangovers, it's time to drink water, get a little sun in your eyes, and reflect on how far you've come and remind yourself how far you've got to go. Your project is live. There is work in the world that wasn't there before. It's good work. It's creative work. It sells. At least you hope it does. That leads me to the sixth and final of the 6 Basic Troop Leading Steps, **Supervise**.

This final step is the most important step of all six. If you don't supervise and something goes wrong, you better be prepared to point your finger without a knife hand. Better yet, don't even point it and just raise your hand. If you're the account lead, it falls on you. Once you get to that level, it doesn't all of the sudden fall on you. You've got to start taking responsibility at every level. Own your work and own your team's efforts. They're your team, but you're their leader. It falls on you.

Supervise your work by checking in with the publications where your client's ad is running. See how they look. Take a snapshot. Inspect it. If it looks good, send it to the team in an email with some words of praise. If you notice something, investigate. If it's cause for alarm, raise that alarm. If you hear a call from the guard house (your client or your vendor), repeat that call to all calls more distant from the guard house than your own. Get help to solve problems. If there are no problems, great! Then celebrate it with another round of drinks at the pub. Follow up and report to your client. Keep them in the loop and start planning for the next one. And the next one, the one after that, and then another one. Do it for two years at a time. Don't go jumping around every 6-9 months. Stick at one place like a tour of duty. 2 years, 4-5 years, or if you find a forever home, then go there and motivate until you run the place. It's an easy game, it's just advertising.

No matter what client you're working on or what kind of campaign it is, the point is, you've gotta look after your work and that means looking after your people. Your people on the agency side, your people on the client side, your people on the vendor side. Look after them all. Make sure they have what they need to win. Then you win. Everybody wins. That means more rounds for everybody at the pub. BAMCIS, damnit.

Chapter 6: Commander's Intent – Clarity will encourage peak performance from the top down

While in basic training, the recruit may learn more in those 90 days than they've learned their entire life. The amount of knowledge they drill into your brain in between long bouts of actual drill movements on the parade deck is comparable only to the amount of dark energy is in the cosmos. I don't know how much that is, but it's gotta be a lot, something like two-thirds of the universe is made of dark matter, isn't it? Perhaps the drill instructors are plugged into the dark matter somehow through an ancient masonic ritual perfected by Captain Samuel L. Nicholas, the First Commandant of Marines (and a known Free and Accepted Mason). Maybe this dark energy is all the Marine Corps knowledge from 244 years of existence, plus the knowledge of every warrior tribe since the dawn of sentient life. It's from this dark energy our motivation is derived once we become Marine. Maybe that's why I have an endless supply of motivation? I don't know why my enthusiasm and gung-ho spirit has stuck around since basic training. Maybe it's because I never had the misfortune of being jaded by PTSD wounds inflicted by the theaters of combat. Maybe it's because I find true value in the teachings of this family of brothers and sisters. A family approaching one quarter of one millennium in its traditions of excellence in leadership.

Think about that for a minute, the Marine Corps has only been around for one quarter of one thousand years. It sounds like a long time, but there have been warrior classes that have been around for thousands more. The aborigines in Australia have been teaching the same fighting traditions for millennium, plural. The Zulu nation has a steep tradition of warriors. Sparta's reign lasted about a thousand years. The Marine Corps, in its youth, has become known as one of the fiercest fighting organizations of this planet. How did we get here? We read our history. In our history, not just U.S. history, but our warrior history, there are countless stories of leaders and commanders exemplifying the basic leadership principles I learned in basic training with the Marines. Among Marines, our lodestars include names like, Smedley Butler, Chesty Puller, Opha May Johnson, John Basilone, Dan Daly, and others. I'll leave you to look up their accomplishments and their histories on your own, because Google is a wonderful thing. What I will tell you is that in each one of these Marines and in other cultures of battle tested warriors, there is a sure understanding about the vital importance of a concept we call, "The Commander's Intent."

These leaders must have access to that dark energy, too, because from them one hears legends of vitality, strength, and feats that demonstrate a kind esprit de corps that is nothing short of legendary. They are giants among giants. They are true to form leaders with every fiber of their being. They are capable of legendary feats because of two things:

1) they or their Commander has an unshakeable confidence in both themselves and their team, and 2) they or their team has an unshakable confidence in their Commander's Intent. This intent must permeate the being of every leader from the top brass Generals down to the Private First Class in charge of the poor and near hopeless Privates. (If you don't get in trouble, you'll only stay Private for 6-9 months, all things must pass).

When a group of warriors gather to accomplish a task and complete confidence in the commander's intent is fully realized--everything else falls into place.

I'm looking for warriors to join me and the handful of other military minds I've met in this advertising business that understand the value of clearly communicating the Commander's Intent.

I am such a fanatic about this particular issue, because when leadership is exemplified from the top then the rest of the organization has a beacon in the darkness to follow, and it's dark out there, dear motivators, and the night is full of terrors. So much of business has been about shareholder value among the giant holding companies that the truly creative nature of this business often gets squashed or squandered due to a lack of leadership. There is an effective way to drive shareholder value that organizations are only now starting to realize, it isn't all about profit, it's all about people.

When troop morale is up, when the people are happy and when they feel fulfilled, they perform. That goes for the people on your team and the people your team serve. As a leader, your entire obsession should be around service. Service to your team first, because more often than not, it's your team that will service your customer.

In the discipline of Account Management, or Client Service, or whatever you want to call it, it's about relationships. The most critical relationship in advertising is often the client facing touch point for the business and more often than not, it's the account executive on the day-to-day business and a more senior account director or group account director leading the relationship with the top client on the client side. Depending on the size of the account, there may be two or three account executives, two or three account supervisors, one or two management supervisors, and one account director and one group account director. It really all depends.

No matter the size of the operation, there is always an objective. How do we solve a particular problem for our clients? The objective rests at a distant (or not so distant) place in spacetime. I like to think of the objective as the veritable peak of a mountain top. A Commander's vision, from the junior account executive running a client status meeting with senior creatives, strategists, and production teams, or from the CMO of an agency leading a multi-million-dollar pitch, the vision and intent of the commander must be palpable to everyone involved. How does the junior account executive or the CMO know what the commander's intent is? The commander must express their intent regularly and with consistency. The intent must be inherent in each member of the team. For my time at McCann, it was "Truth Well Told." At Ogilvy, at first it was "Creativity & Effectiveness," and it evolved into "Make Brands Matter." At Madras Global, our intent is "Brand Commerce."

Now what do all these things mean at a glance? Nothing to the layman. To the employee, they are everything. The lifeblood of the agency. Why we exist. We exist to fulfill the commander's intent.

What is the commander's intent of McCann? "To tell the truth and to tell it well." To study your client's mission, vision, and values for their brand so voraciously that you know it better than your client themselves. To understand the vital truths that make up the brand and to tell a story to the world so compelling to the world that the story does its job--it sells.

What is the commander's intent of Ogilvy? "To make brands matter." Without proper context, it's meaningless, but to those who report to the hallowed halls of The Chocolate Factory in Hell's Kitchen and the other Ogilvy offices around the world, "to make brands matter" is to take responsibility for the stewardship we've been entrusted to carry on for these brands. To help our clients with these multi-million-dollar budgets spend their money wisely, and communicate messages that mean something to the public. To communicate in a way that elevates the brand from just a provider of a product to a genuine steward of a lifestyle. To make the brand matter to one person enough. To make it matter so much that they take the money out of their wallet and buy something.

At Madras Global, as a Client Service Director (I've since moved on to become a Strategic Advisor for the agency, on occasion), I had the honor of running stewardship for several brands I love, and for each one of them, I took the commander's intent of "Brand Commerce" and applied that intent to may daily decisions and general approach toward my clients and my team. We do everything we can to make sure that when a client invests their brand and marketing dollars with us, we will work with the brand to improve upon those commercial moments with the brand. Those moments of commerce. Every touchpoint for every brand should have a connection to commerce, and commerce comes from connection first, but that's a topic for another book.

If you enter a company that does a poor job expressing the

commander's intent, it's likely due to a clear lack of leadership. Pay attention before you take the job and make sure there is at least some semblance of leadership. One may never know until you step inside the actual rodeo, but you owe it to yourself to do your homework. Look up the Twitter handles of the leaders within the organizations you aspire to work for. You don't need to join a big institution like I did. Those giants often do a great job at employee onboarding with messages expressing the history of the company, the commanders that led to their success, and the current intent for the day. You might start at a smaller shop or a mid-size shop. Look into those leaders on LinkedIn if they're not expressive on Twitter. See if they write and make an attempt at thought leadership. Pay attention to their words. Words are the bricks and mortar of an organization's morale. If the words to describe an organization are full of hot air or buzzwords that make it unclear what they're all about, steer clear of those mother truckers.

Once inside the organization, no matter what role you take, live that commander's intent. Breathe it. Every day. Day in and day out. Be the company man, but be a maverick. Don't just fall in line. Fully adapt to and adopt the core values of the organization. Ogilvy was a great place to do this for me because David Ogilvy truly is one of the greatest leaders in the history of this business. The Learning & Development Office at Ogilvy, along with the HR department, had no short supply of literature and resources for me to draw upon. There are countless whitepapers to read about the thought leadership that Ogilvy provides to the industry and their clients. The books by David Ogilvy are masterclass works of business literature. The training programs one may enroll in providing truckloads of information about how to adopt the timeless principles of direct marketing to the modern digital world.

Ogilvy also wrote a pamphlet about the core values and principles he lived by as a leader and he wished for his employees and partners at Ogilvy to live by them, as well. This document I carried around in the breast pocket of my blazer, every day, once I discovered it existed. Every once in a while, I'd pull it out and read aloud in my commanding voice, the words of a man rife with fear that his company would be lost to the idolatries of Sir Martin Sorrell and the rest of his bean counters at WPP. I'll tell you that as a 5-year veteran of Ogilvy from 2012 to 2017, I saw more of WPP in Ogilvy than I saw of Ogilvy in Ogilvy, but there are others like me who still carry on his torch and with a passion. Shelly Lazarus did amazing things in her time there, but that was a generation before my time. While I was there, leadership transitioned from Miles Young to John Seifert. Both men I came to know and admire and had the good fortune of making time with each of them on several occasions of varying capacities.

John Seifert awarded me the Diversity & Inclusion Champion award in

2015 for my enthusiasm for the Professional Networks at Ogilvy. This was the same year I co-founded Salute, the Military Veterans Network with my Marine buddy and A/V tech at Ogilvy, Sam Ware. Semper Fidelis, brother. My fellow colleagues and partners at Ogilvy voted me, the white-cisgender and hopelessly heterosexual male, because I simply was the loudest voice for diversity. This wasn't an award given to me by an executive team. My partners voted for me. That moment on stage next to John, after sitting with him in a handful of Professional Network meetings, was one of the proudest moments of my time at Ogilvy. I was standing next to the top man and he stood there and shook my hand, smiling and beaming with pride. It didn't hurt that his father was a United States Marine.

Before he retired, I gave Miles Young one of the one hundred challenge coins I minted during my time at the helm of Salute while at Ogilvy. The only reason I think Miles liked me is that he gave instructions to an HR lead on a Thursday to participate in the Hudson River Games event. The event was on Saturday. I walked around the halls and recruited 10 friends and folks I reached out to over the course of that afternoon and the following day. We didn't win, but we had a helluva time and I ended up on New York News 1 that day. Next time I'm in London, I'm aiming to stop by the New School at Oxford to see if he is indeed keeping the memento on his desk, as he told me he would when I gave it to him. He told me it would be one of his most prized possessions he'd take with him from his office in New York. He is a voracious student of history and his knowledge of the revolution is unparalleled by most Americans I know, especially of the voyage of the Marquis de Lafayette across the Atlantic to provide the much-needed reinforcements for Washington. Ogilvy was a Francophile and his wife is on the board of trustees for the living museum that is that boat. I had the pleasure of joining Mr. Young and even caught a glance of Herta, Ogilvy's wife. It was quite an experience.

These are the experiences you'll enjoy, too, if you live into the Commander's Intent. I'm talking about THE Commander. I'm talking about your heart and its connection to source, whatever source or higher power that may be for you. God. The Cosmos. The is. Or just your own internal compass. No one should ever command you to do anything you don't want to do. A good Commander never really commands anyway, they simply have no shortage of motivated, dedicated, hard-charging volunteers. Find yourself a good Commander and win. Look into their outfit and jump on board. Keep it one hundred, as those kids say. Those kids will follow you, too, because you've got the vision like the commander above you and the commander above them all the way to the top. Sooner or later, you'll find that you're The Commander and the only person you report to is yourself and your obligation to serve those that follow you. That's the spot to be, if you can take it, dear motivator. I know you can...so go out there and get it.

Chapter 7: Advertising is a Battlefield – Every plan goes to hell when the first shots are fired

You know the saying, once shots are fired, the plan is moot and people just start playing in survival mode. Reactionary leadership is better than no leadership, but the best leadership has a plan for when the plan goes south, and a plan for when the back-up plan doesn't work. I never experienced the battle joys of combat, so I never had to worry about a grave and fatal outcome if our client's ambitions didn't work out. The worst that could happen is when a client will let the agency go. There are always more clients. So, it's easy not to take it personal. That said, it hasn't happened to me...yet.

It's always good to remember that it's just advertising...we're not saving lives or defending nations.

When the fog of war does strike on a project, take charge. If there is an angry client or angry team member looking for someone to blame, if you're the account manager and the account lead won't take the blame, just take the blame and offer solutions. People have heard me say, "I blame myself," just about as often as they hear me say, "motivate." You'd be surprised at how many times the situation will diffuse and people will move on just because someone has the courage to take responsibility. Even when your team knows it might not really be your fault, the words themselves, and the action of accepting responsibility in order to move the project forward is often noted. Don't be afraid to hold or call for post-mortems, where a team meets to discuss what went wrong and how to prevent it from happening again.

During the tough times and late nights, volunteer to help out in areas where you might not be expert because sometimes many hands make light work. I've spent many an hour as a junior copywriter, junior producer, junior strategist, and junior print production manager, especially in those more boutique or small agency environments.

The other thing that is often praised and appreciated is food and drink. Make sure the team is fed. If you're the account manager and you've got the corporate card, use it. Expense lunches, dinners, team drinks during brainstorm sessions, anything you can think of to boost morale. It goes a long way when you're in the trenches. It's tough responding to fire drills into the midnight hours. It's even tougher when you're that hungry angry like in those "You're Not You When You're Hungry" Snickers commercials.

There are all sorts of unexpected issues that arise throughout the day in the beautiful rodeo. An unexpected project that drops out of the blue with 24-48-hour turn-around time. The client wanting to reschedule the shoot because they forgot about their anniversary. Your creative director calling your designer buddy's work an abortion. These moments in advertising are like those times in basic training where you think you're gonna get a great day on the firing range learning to hone your skills with the M-16 A2 Service Rifle, but instead, you get to be in the pit all day doing pushups, mountain climbers, and pull ups in-between hydration bouts that make you have to pee so bad that you've got to emasculate yourself and ask for a head call in between the regularly scheduled bio breaks. The reason that it's emasculating is because the drill instructors will only allow those unscheduled head calls in case of emergencies. Pissing your pants isn't really an emergency, so they get a laugh by having the recruit request for an emergency head call and the script usually goes something like this:

> [Jones stands at attention in between a set of push-ups and mountain climbers]

> Recruit Jones: Recruit Jones requests permission to speak to Drill Instructor Sergeant Liesik, sir!
> Drill Instructor: Speak, but keep doing mountain climbers, recruit. MOUNTAIN CLIMBERS RIGHT NOW.

> [Platoon 3074 proceeds to Mountain Climbers]

> Recruit Jones: Recruit Jones requests permission to make a head call, sir!

Drill Instructor: Denied. Wait for the next bio brake, recruit. PUSH UPS RIGHT NOW!

[Platoon 3074 proceeds with Push Ups]

Recruit Jones: Recruit Jones requests permission to speak to Drill Instructor Sergeant Liesik, sir!

Drill Instructor: What now, recruit?

Recruit Jones: Recruit Jones requests permission to make an emergency head call, sir!

Drill Instructor: It's an emergency, recruit? I don't hear the sirens. MOUNTAIN CLIMBERS RIGHT NOW!

[Platoon 3074 proceeds to Mountain Climbers]

Recruit Jones: Sirens, sir?

Drill Instructor: You said it was an emergency, didn't your recruit?

Recruit Jones: Yes, sir. It's an emergency, sir.

Drill Instructor: Let me hear your best ambulance siren, Jones. RECRUIT HILL, all the way down, damnit!

Recruit Jones: Weeee-oooooo, weeeee-ooooooo, weeeeee-oooooo

Drill Instructor: Louder Jones.

Recruit Jones: WEEEE-OOOOO! WEEEE-OOOOO! WEEEE-OOOOOO!

Drill Instructor: Now I'm convinced it's an emergency. You have 3 minutes to get inside that head and get out. I want to hear that ambulance while you're in that head, Jones. It's an emergency all right. Your fellow recruits will be holding themselves in the push-up position until you get back. Now move! PUSH UP POSITIONS!

Recruits: [moans]

[Jones sirens his way to the barracks for a head call]

[Platoon laughs]

Drill Instructor: NO COMMENTS FROM THE PEANUT GALLERY THIS IS AN EMERGENCY!

[Drill Instructor pulls cover down over face to head his laughter and loss of bearing from the rest of the recruits]

Fin

Comical? Yeah, it is. Especially when you consider the fact that we're all doing this instead of firing rounds down range because JONES didn't stamp his towel with his ID number on the proper side of the towel and the drill instructor noticed that morning. Let's say I wasn't the favorite recruit of the platoon that day. If I recall, I missed the instruction on stamping the towel the day prior due to being out on a medical mission (going to the doctor was called a mission, because everything is a mission in basic training). My squad leader at the time rushed me through the set-up of the foot locker and personal effects at the foot of the rack (or bed for you civilian motivators out there). He showed me his set-up and told me to mirror it. Easy enough, but I didn't pay close enough attention to the way the towel was stamped and hung in a particular manner so that when I hung my towel the number wasn't centered properly or was upside down or something. It was something trivial, but it was enough to set the drill instructor off. Or, maybe it was that our range time got pushed for some "per the need of the Marine Corps" and an active unit needed the range time to prepare for deployment. Or maybe it was that the Drill Instructors found out that their good buddies died in Fallujah that week and they just wanted to take out their frustrations by slaying us in the pit. Who knows what it was that put them on a tear? We recruits had to adapt.

If it wasn't me that week, it was someone else. They were just messing with us. The point is, when advertising starts throwing its own trials and tribulations at you and clients are firing their friendly fire at you, as they sometimes do, or the competition hits the client with a metaphorical IED (improvised explosive device for those civilians that hasn't paid attention to the news headlines since 2003 and don't know what an IED is) and you've gotta roll with those punches. Sometimes it'll be out of your hands and you and your team gotta dig into that foxhole and wait out the battle until air support comes through. The one thing you must remember, the one thing you must never forget, through any moment of adversity, is that all things must pass and *this too shall pass*.

That mindset, a mindset that says, "this too shall pass," is reminiscent of the classic song by George Harrison, from which this phrase, "all things must pass" became popular when he released his triple album by the same title. In it, he hauntingly sings the lyrics with all the gravity of his own mortality weighing upon each line he utters and with each strum, he strings, "seems my love is up and has left you with no warning, it's not always going to be this grey."

While it might be interpreted as a breakup song (because many great songs are about falling in love or falling out of it), it could just as likely be the song George wrote to help his loved ones cope with his own mortality. George is known for saying: "Death is just where your suit falls off and now, you're in your other suit. You can't see it on this level, but it's alright. Don't worry." While he obviously can't force his dearest and nearest not to worry, because we each are all free and independent human beings, he sure could write a song. That's what I think, "All Things Must Pass" is really about...confrontation with the fact that even the good must come to an end. So it goes with the bad...because--*all things must pass.*

The phrase, 'this too shall pass" is a Persian adage made famous in the West by an English poet they called, Edward FitzGerald. Before the West caught wind of such wisdom, Attar of Nishapur, a Persian poet, recorded the fable "...of a powerful king who asks assembled wise men to create a ring that will make him happy when he is sad. After deliberation the sages hand him a simple ring with the Persian words "This too shall pass" etched on it, which has the desired effect to make him happy when he is sad. It also, however, became a curse for whenever he is happy."

While I haven't been on a true to form battlefield with bullets flying, I've spent over 10 years in the trenches of advertising and the bullets aren't that life-threatening kind, but they're the career threatening kind. In those situations, it's key to remember, "all things must pass, so this too shall pass."

As all things must pass, so must this chapter, but before I do, please know that I've experienced a sense of liberation since I've accepted this view of temporality in nearly everything I witness. Nothing remains the same. Should I be fortunate enough to enjoy their love my entire life, however many phases that love may live in, my own love will "up and leave one day without warning." Our mortal coils are bound to expire. No one gets out of this life alive. Except those that realize that death is an illusion and that the shedding of the mortal coil is nothing but a transition from one conscious container of sentience to another.

As we make our way through these various roles and responsibilities we garner throughout our years, those positions, too, must pass. As much as I loved running Salute and the Military Veterans Network at Ogilvy, I had to leave to evolve and ultimately do what's best for my family. So, may it be with you and your career, dear motivator. Don't let it get you down. Just stay after it. In the field of battle, the night is darkest before the dawn. The only way to make it through the battlefield is by taking it chow to chow and to remember that when everything goes wrong that all things pass, and this, too, shall pass. No matter where your battlefield is, keep your head on a swivel, look after your brothers and sisters, and remember there will always be time for chow or a nap to be had so that robot can refuel and recharge. That mindset is all it takes to win, because the other half the battle is won just by showing up.

Chapter 8 Warriors are Non-Binary – People are people, that's it, let them fight their best fight

I talk a lot about robots. That much goes without saying. That said, dear motivator, I also write about robots, as you've seen from Chapter 3. I don't just write words about robots, I write poetry. Have a look at this one I wrote about 8 years ago:

> *Binary or Not* • 20110507
> Systematic interpretation of intention
> systematically initiates the invention of software systems
> with demonstrable operational efficiency.
>
> It's not exciting, settle down.
>
> Nestle down and excuse the scenery.
> It's not as quiet outside as it is in here.
>
> These machines are manifesting awareness.
>
> The bareness of our intention is interpreted by them–
> they think us careless.
> I couldn't care less.
>
> In fairness, the entire notion is ridiculous.
>
> What's theirs, what's ours, no longer holds.
> No place in our town will turn away a robot.
>
> Binary or not, a spot's a spot on this rowboat.

So, I'm no Robert Frost, okay. I get it. The point I'm aiming to land here is that life is but a dream and we're all rowing this rowboat together. There is a spot for everybody to help row, I don't care if you're a robot, or an android, or a person, or a Pleiadean (what's up, fam). I don't care if you're black, white, brown, yellow, pink, or purple. I don't care where you fall on the gender spectrum. I don't care who you wanna bone or how you wanna bone when you're boning. What I care about is how hard you row that boat. How do you row my boat? You bring ideas. You are the ideas you bring to the table. Not the color of your skin or the gender you identify with. Bring me a good idea and I'll love you forever.

There is no doubt in my mind that agencies are some of the more progressive places for this type of mindset. That's one reason I love the industry is that it genuinely feels like a bunch of misplaced misfits. There is no shortage of diversity. We're all creative types, whether or not we work on the creative floors. Well at least, I like to think we're all creative, whether or not we work in the creative departments. Just like that warrior spirit lives in our hearts, our creative spirit resides there, too. When we quiet our minds and listen to that creative heart, it speaks wonders. Whether it be how artfully you craft a contact report or a line of copy, or how cleverly you produce a TV spot, or how creatively you pivot your tables in your spreadsheets, you end up being creative. You can't help it. The agency will rub off on you and you on it, no matter what kind of robot you're rocking, operating system you're running, or how ever big your warrior heart happens to be.

I'd like to respectfully request my brothers and sisters, my fellow passengers on this great spaceship Earth, to understand I am clearly a white man, and spent most of my life, arguably all of it, free from discrimination. I do my best to befriend anyone willing to trade stories. I love stories. I love stories that have great ideas or truth in them. Those stories come from every passenger on this planet. Those stories come from every person from every country and every tribe under the sun. Every passenger has perception. Every passenger has a perspective.

I've heard stories of all sorts of discrimination and abuse of power against people unable to adequately defend themselves. It makes me seethe when I hear it. I won't tolerate bigotry or harassment if I see it. Because I'm fortunate enough to know what it's like to live and work with the respect of generally everybody I encounter, I wish for everyone to have the same experience to enjoy, if they wish it.

It just takes a bit of effort to be a human to other humans. They're all just being human as best they know how. Everybody and their robot has a spot on my rowboat. Me and my robot like other motivated operators like us that respect other robots and their operators. My mind doesn't judge another mind based off the type of robot their rocking. Nor does my heart judge another heart based upon the type of paint job that surrounds that heart.

Pigmentation is not a reflection of intelligence or capability. Period. Sexual preference is not a reflection of intelligence or capability. Period. Religious preference is not a reflection of intelligence or capability. Period. What matters in the business of advertising most is ideas. It's an industry that is worse than some but better than most in accepting the LGBTQ communities.

At Ogilvy in New York, I spent 5 years active in the Young Professional Network and founded and led Salute, the Military Professional Network for two years. Those were just two of 10 networks all devoted to affiliate groups, including the Women's Leadership, Ogilvy Doonya for Muslim employees, Black Diaspora Professional Network, Working Parents Network, LatinRED, Ogilvy Pride (LGBT), RedLotus (Asia Pacific) and Administrative Professional Network. All these networks brought diverse ideas from every aspect of culture in the business. These networks were run by motivated employees across the NY office, across the U.S., and when I left, expanded into the UK and beyond.

Those networks gave me some of the best Ogilvy had to offer. Outside of my usual remit, I learned from attending the YPN events that these organizations were all run by volunteers. I put up my hand for the Young Professional Network (YPN) in 2012 when I moved to NY as a single man. For obvious reasons, I aimed to meet ladies outside of my chain of command that could introduce me to their friends in the city. I never really believed in dating within the office, but I won't lie, there were one or two ladies that may have captured my attention before I met my wife on the corner of Prince and Mulberry one summer evening in 2013.

I grew to love YPN for other reasons as I grew older. It's funny, the same thing happened to me with poetry and guitar. I picked both up in my adolescence because I thought I would woo my way to any woman's heart. After my fair share rejection from the fairer sex, I grew to love the spoken word and playing all sorts of instruments for their own independent bits of beauty, not just because some ladies find it fancy.

As the ripe old age of 35 approached, I knew my tenure with the Young Professional Network wouldn't last much longer until I was, 'that old guy that likes to hang around the interns,' so I obviously couldn't have that continue for much longer. I didn't see any affiliation in any other network, so I asked around about starting a military network. It got a lot of positive reception from all sorts of folks. One day, at Landmark Tavern, the landmark pub next to Ogilvy there in Hell's Kitchen, my good friend Melissa told me that I should report to Donna Pedro, because I would be starting Salute the next quarter. She said it with a wink and a smile, meaning that all I had to do was follow through, because she teed it up for me with her boss, the Chief Diversity & Inclusion officer, Donna Pedro.

Not one to shy away from an opportunity to meet with the Chief Executive Officer of Ogilvy USA once a quarter, as is tradition for the leaders of each network, I took my voluntold duties with the utmost enthusiasm. Why not? It'd be a great way to find out about what other veterans were in the building. I knew that most all veterans bleed green, they don't see gender or race as an issue, because when you're training for war, you rely on your brothers and sisters to survive. Those issues suddenly don't matter in the face of mortality.

Sitting around a table of 10-12 leaders of all these networks and listening to an industry giant like John Seifert talk for 10-15 minutes once a quarter made all five years of my time there at Ogilvy invaluable. Each time we stepped in the room with him, it was a master class for me in the type of language a CEO at that level uses among his partners and with his teams.

One thing Mr. Seifert reiterated constantly is this (and I paraphrase here): "You are the veritable backbone of culture in this agency. Each of you and your networks represent the diversity across our organization and you, of all my teams, have a unique ability to carry this message forward: we are one Ogilvy and we will find our way forward and continue to adapt as the landscape transforms before us. Ogilvy isn't going anywhere and it's thanks to the talent and tenacity that each of you and the groups you represent bring to our company."

I truly think that Donna Pedro and John Seifert are two of the leaders in the industry that are driving that commitment to diversity and inclusion forward. In my time there, I took many notes on how to champion diversity and I intend to continue doing so for the rest of my career, no matter what industry I'm in.

People are people. Warriors are non-binary. Let them fight their best fight and you'll never lack for ideas.

Chapter 9: Beans, Bullets, and Bandages – Logistics, troop morale, and the devil in the details

The term "beans and bullets" came into common vernacular during the Civil War. In the 20th century, they added, "bandages," to care for the sick and wounded. For advertising, beans, bullets and bandages remains somewhat the same. Allow me to illustrate…

Beans represents food. Keep your team fed. Make sure that they are able to break away for lunch and if they can't offer to go buy them lunch. Make sure if they have to come in early then they have donuts or bacon egg and cheese sammys waiting for them with hot coffee on the side. Make sure you've got the sugars and the Splendas and the creams and the oat milks and all that jazz. Serve the team and they'll serve the work.

Bullets are not the rounds down range but rather the bullet points in your presentations outlining your meeting's agenda. You need hot slides with sweet bullets that reveal the aim for each meeting to show how the agency is about to lower costs or increase revenue with some dope creative ideas and ad like objects to follow those bullets. The creative work is the air support, the A-10 Warthogs, the C-130s, the CH-53s, the CH-46s, the F-18s, the Harriers...you know, the sexy stuff. Death from above.

Bandages are the booze, the brews, baked goods, Best Buy gift cards (or better yet, Amazon [or better yet, preloaded AmEx Debit Cards]). Bandages are the things you buy to make your team feel better for having to call their wife to let them know they'll be missing the kid's rehearsal for the third time. You've gotta make sure you make good. Flex that expense account if you've got a corporate card. Get thrifty and manage up, if you don't have one yourself. Do your best to manage timelines so this doesn't happen.

Managing timelines is tough, especially with tough clients. The trick is to earn their trust. Don't go pushing for more time, every time. Only when it counts. When you do push for more time, push for great creative work. Make the wait worth it.

Find the person on your team that does and make best friends. Then get them to flex that expense account. Flex it until the corporate overlords tell you to stop flexing it. It goes a long way to keep up morale when you keep the team fed, caffeinated, and boozed up at night after the work is done. Take care of that team.

Most importantly, remember that the superior fire power is what win wars. If the team isn't fed well enough to throw rounds accurately down range, you're gonna have problems. Make sure you nurture their aim and keep them well fed. If the team isn't feeling well enough to throw rounds accurately down range, you're gonna have problems. Make sure you nurture their wounds and get them back on the battlefield where they may aim true. If the team doesn't have the necessary equipment to throw rounds down range (like working laptops, ready for issue phones, working Internet, and whiteboards, presentation boards, or what have you), then you're gonna have problems. Make sure you look after the equipment and that everything is in working order. You don't want to see the kind of pandemonium that happens when the coffee machine breaks on a creative floor. Or any floor for that matter. Don't ever let a creative go without a powerful machine.

Make sure you've got all sorts of bullets. Each role has its varying capacity. You can't win a war with a whole bunch of shotguns and revolvers. You need access to all the different types of rounds to throw down range. You need battle rifles, sniper rifles, tanks, artillery, rocket propelled grenade launchers, hand grenades, non-lethal rounds, rounds that aren't even rounds, like those fancy electromagnetic beams the military has now. Air superiority is crucial, almost more so than the seas, both is best. Don't forget your cyberspace weapons. Oh, and the Space Corps. If you have the means, I highly recommend you pick one up. You might not need to have all of these at the same time to go to war, but over the course of a war, you'll find you can make a weapon out of just about anything.

In basic training, during our Marine Corps Martial Arts training, our instructors made sure to stress the importance of identifying weapons of opportunity. When you run out of bullets, fixing bayonets isn't always an option. You've gotta look around and make do with what you've got. In an agency, sometimes that means making a junior copywriter out of an account executive, or a junior strategist out of an account director, or a producer out of a project manager. Sometimes a well-placed can of beans will knock out your opponent just as well as a bullet will put out the lights. If the opponent is unconscious, that's still a win, right? If my client's brand still sells more products than their competitors, it's still a win, right?

These days, brand building budgets are slim, especially among outdoor retailers like Cabela's. When I worked on that account, they focused the majority of their efforts on promotions and seasonal sales with price heavy copy and a large print budget for their various catalogues. When my clients asked my team to come up with low-budget video posts for their Facebook page, we came up with an idea for user generated content. We designed a one-page PDF that outlined how to hold a small American flag in-front of your phone, in portrait mode, and have a backdrop of a beautiful and scenic outdoor location to celebrate the outdoors on the 4th of July. We sent 100 of these kits, complete with little flags, and a neatly designed PDF with instructions, to friends and family around the country. We sourced footage from all over the place, waterfalls, oceans, mountains, fields, streams, hills, forests, and rivers, and any kind of land you can imagine to serve as the backdrop to Old Glory, our Grand Old Flag, the colors that just won't run, our Red White and Blue.

Once we tied all the footage together, we needed a music bed. The client couldn't even afford the rights to purchase a fully produced song, so what did we do? I brought in my Taylor guitar, the very same that carried me through many solo performances on stage in Okinawa Japan later in my Marine Corps tenure, the same guitar that I wrote sad songs on for my lady across the ocean, the same 710ce that I love and care for even to this day, I dipped into a phone booth on the 10th floor of that Chocolate Factory and I plucked a single note melody of 'America the Beautiful' and recorded it on my iPhone 6s.

I shipped that tune to my editor buddy, a fella even taller than me, and he laid it over all the beautiful American footage. Among our friends and family, my sister ended up with the first clip and my dad ended up with the last one. There were dozens of clips from other friends and family of the team in between, one for almost every note. It's one of my favorite bits of work we've ever produced. Including the client's ad buy for some social boost, we did it for less than 9 thousand dollars. It went on to be one of the most successful social posts Cabela's ever deployed on Facebook. I'd be curious to see how it stands these days.

Get at me Bass Pro Shops, let a brother know those details?

Chapter 10: The Few, The Proud, The Traits – 14 Leadership Traits from the best of the best

In this and the following chapter, I'm going to get right to the fundamentals.

First, we'll cover the 14 Leadership Traits. We'll give the definition, significance, and example, per our reference MCTP 6-10B, Appendix A. It's word for word. These words not only inspired me in my tenure as a Marine, but during my ten-year career in advertising.

I hope they will continue to inspire Marines, veterans, ROTC students, and anyone interested in exemplifying these traits in advertising. Traits one earns by employing the 11 Leadership Principles, which we'll cover in the following chapter. A unit with true leadership is a unit that runs with the ever illustrious, *esprit de corps*.

These traits and principles are not just something individuals may take into their respective professional fields. Brand managers should consider how to weave these principles and traits into their brand experiences. Brands that stand for something are brands that are getting noticed and that garner loyalty among their fanbase. Why not have your brand stand for the same traits that the few and the proud stand for? Let's review and wonder, shall we?

The following language is all pulled directly from MCTP 6-10B, Appendix A.

The 14 Leadership Traits of the United States Marine Corps:

I. **BEARING**

    A. Definition. Creating a favorable impression in carriage, appearance, and personal conduct at all times.

    B. Significance. The ability to look, act, and speak like a leader whether or not these manifestations indicate one's true feelings. Some signs of these traits are clear and plain speech, an erect gait, and impeccable personal appearance.

    C. Example. Wearing clean, pressed uniforms, and shining boots and brass. Avoiding profane and vulgar language. Keeping a trim, fit appearance. Keeping your head, keeping your word and keeping your temper.

II. **COURAGE**

    A. Courage is a mental quality that recognizes fear of danger or criticism, but enables a Marine to proceed in the face of it with calmness and firmness.

B. Significance. Knowing and standing for what is right, even in the face of popular disfavor, is often the leader's lot. The business of fighting and winning wars is a dangerous one; the importance of courage on the battlefield is obvious.

C. Example. Accepting criticism for making subordinates field day for an extra hour to get the job done correctly.

III. **DECISIVENESS**

A. Definition. Ability to make decisions promptly and to announce them in a clear, forceful manner.

B. Significance. The quality of character which guides a person to accumulate all available facts in a circumstance, weigh the facts, choose and announce an alternative which seems best. It is often better that a decision be made promptly than a potentially better one be made at the expense of more time.

C. Example. A leader who sees a potentially dangerous situation developing, immediately takes action to prevent injury from occurring. For example, if he/she sees a unit making a forced march along a winding road without road guards posted, he/she should immediately inform the unit leader of the oversight, and if senior to that unit leader, direct that proper precautions be taken.

IV. **DEPENDABILITY**

   A. Definition. The certainty of proper performance of duty.

   B. Significance. The quality which permits a senior to assign a task to a junior with the understanding that it will be accomplished with minimum supervision. This understanding includes the assumption that the initiative will be taken on small matters not covered by instructions.

   C. Example. The squad leader ensures that his/her squad falls out in the proper uniform without having been told to by the platoon sergeant. The staff officer, who hates detailed, tedious paperwork, yet makes sure the report meets his/her and his/her supervisor's standards before having it leave his desk.

V. ENDURANCE

A. Definition. The mental and physical stamina measured by the ability to withstand pain, fatigue, stress, and hardship.

B. Significance. The quality of withstanding pain during a conditioning hike in order to improve stamina is crucial in the development of leadership. Leaders are responsible for leading their units in physical endeavors and for motivating them as well.

C. Example. A Marine keeping up on a 10-mile forced march even though he/she has blisters on both feet and had only an hour of sleep the previous night. An XO who works all night to ensure that promotion/pay problems are corrected as quickly as humanly possible because he/she realizes that only through this effort can one of his/her Marines receive badly needed back-pay the following morning.

VI. INITIATIVE

A. Definition. Taking action in the absence of orders.

B. Significance. Since an NCO often works without close supervision, emphasis is placed on being a self-starter. Initiative is a founding principle of Marine Corps Warfighting philosophy.

C. Example. In the unexplained absence of the platoon sergeant, an NCO takes charge of the platoon and carries out the training schedule.

VII. **ENTHUSIASM**

A. Definition. The display of sincere interest and exuberance in the performance of duty.

B. Significance. Displaying interest in a task, and an optimism that it can be successfully completed, greatly enhances the likelihood that the task will be successfully completed.

C. Example. A Marine who leads a chant or offers to help carry a load that is giving someone great difficulty while on a hike despite being physically tired himself, encourages his fellow Marines to persevere.

VIII. **INTEGRITY**

A. Definition. Uprightness of character and soundness of moral principles. The quality of truthfulness and honesty.

B. Significance. A Marine's word is his/her bond. Nothing less than complete honesty in all of your dealings with subordinates, peers, and superiors is acceptable.

C. Example. A Marine who uses the correct technique on the obstacle course, even when he/she cannot be seen by the evaluator. During an inspection, if something goes wrong or is not corrected as had been previously directed, he/she can be counted upon to always respond truthfully and honestly.

IX. **JUDGMENT**

A. Definition. The ability to weigh facts and possible courses of action in order to make sound decisions.

B. Significance. Sound judgment allows a leader to make appropriate decisions in the guidance and training of his/her Marines and the employment of his/her unit. A Marine who exercises good judgment weighs pros and cons accordingly to arrive at an appropriate decision/take proper action.

C. Example. A Marine properly apportions his/her liberty time in order to relax as well as to study.

X. **JUSTICE**

    A. Definition. Giving reward and punishment according to the merits of the case in question. The ability to administer a system of rewards and punishments impartially and consistently.

    B. Significance. The quality of displaying fairness and impartiality is critical in order to gain the trust and respect of subordinates and maintain discipline and unit cohesion, particularly in the exercise of responsibility as a leader.

    C. Example. Fair apportionment of tasks by a squad leader during all field days. Having overlooked a critical piece of evidence which resulted in the unjust reduction of an NCO in a highly publicized incident, the CO sets the punishment aside and restores him to his previous grade even though he knows it will displease his seniors or may reflect negatively on his fitness report. (Also, an example of courage.)

XI. **KNOWLEDGE**

    A. Definition. Understanding of a science or an art. The range of one's information, including professional knowledge and an understanding of your Marines.

    B. Significance. The gaining and retention of current developments in military and naval science and world affairs is important for your growth and development.

    C. Example. The Marine who not only knows how to maintain and operate his assigned weapon, but also knows how to use the other weapons and equipment in the unit.

XII. **LOYALTY**

    A. Definition. The quality of faithfulness to country, the Corps, and unit, and to one's seniors, subordinates, and peers.

    B. Significance. The motto of our Corps is Semper Fidelis, Always Faithful. You owe unswerving loyalty up and down the chain of command: to seniors, subordinates, and peers.

    C. Example. A Marine displaying enthusiasm in carrying out an order of a senior, though he may privately disagree with it. The order may be to conduct a particularly dangerous patrol. The job has to be done, and even if the patrol leader disagrees, he must impart confidence and enthusiasm for the mission to his men.

XIII. **TACT**

    A. Definition. The ability to deal with others without creating hostility.

    B. Significance. The quality of consistently treating peers, seniors, and subordinates with respect and courtesy is a sign of maturity. Tact allows commands, guidance, and opinions to be expressed in a constructive and beneficial manner. This deference must be extended under all conditions regardless of true feelings.

    C. Example. A Marine discreetly points out a mistake drill to an NCO by waiting until after the unit has been dismissed and privately asking which of the two methods are correct, He/she anticipates that the NCO will realize the correct method when shown, and later provide correct instruction to the unit.

XIV. **UNSELFISHNESS**

    A. Definition. Avoidance of providing for one's own comfort and personal advancement at the expense of others.

B. Significance. The quality of looking out for the needs of your subordinates before your own is the essence of leadership. This quality is not to be confused with putting these matters ahead of the accomplishment of the mission.

C. Example. An NCO ensures all members of his unit have eaten before he does, or if water is scarce, he will share what he has and ensure that others do the same. Another example occurs frequently when a Marine receives a package of food from home: the delicacies are shared with everyone in the squad. Yet another form of unselfishness involves the time of the leader. If a Marine needs extra instruction or guidance, the leader is expected to make his/her free time available whenever a need arises.

Chapter 11: On Principles - Employ 11 Leadership Principles to gain morale and *esprit de corps*

Here in the eleventh chapter, let's take a moment to remember the eleventh hour of the eleventh day of the eleventh month in the year nineteen hundred eighteen of our Lord. The eleventh day of November will always have a special place in my heart. Not only because of the celebration that week represents, the Armistice of the First Great War, but it is the day after the Marine Corps Birthday. A day where I like to be with one or more Marines, toasting to the heroes and legends of the Marine Corps and to the battles they waged, both in the theater of combat, and on the front of equality.

While I'm usually nursing a hangover that day, I am still grateful for every man and woman I meet in uniform or that I know is an active or former service member. I love seeing them, whether I just met them that day, or years before, I give a hearty smile and thanks for their service. I love Veterans Day almost as much as I love the Marine Corps Birthday. I don't know how many other days I love as much as those two days, outside of the birth of my children and the day I married my wife.

I promised to get back to the fundamentals, because they are what made me. I'll keep this chapter short, and to the point. Employ these leadership principles, no matter what discipline or domain you go into in marketing or advertising, and any colleague or client, from nearly any industry, would be happy to have you on their team. Here they are, in all their simple glory:

The 11 Marine Corps Leadership Principles (MCTP 6-10B, Appendix B) are:

1. Know yourself and seek self-improvement
2. Be technically and tactically proficient
3. Know your Marines and look out for their welfare
4. Keep your Marines informed
5. Set the example
6. Ensure the task is understood, supervised, and accomplished
7. Train your Marines as a team
8. Make sound and timely decisions
9. Develop a sense of responsibility among your subordinates
10. Employ your command in accordance with its capabilities
11. Seek responsibility and take responsibility for your actions

Be motivating to each other my friends. Employ these principles in your daily life and watch your team turn their heads in shock and awe.

Chapter 12: Shock and Awe, Recruit! Enthusiasm motivates the most, so keep it up

I've been known to use the phrase "Motivate," to express my enthusiasm for anything from excitement for a promotion or work anniversary or when I see great work produced by my team. Have a look at what the Marine Corps delivers from their leadership manual (MCTP 6-10B) regarding motivation:

Motivation answers the "why" of why Marines fight. It also answers the "why" of everything Marines do to prepare for combat. Motivation is based on psychological factors such as needs, desires, impulses, inner drives, impelling forces or commitments that influence the reactions and attitudes of individuals and moves them to action. Simply put for a Marine, motivation is commitment which is generally based on pride and unit integrity.

For example, each of us was motivated to join the Marine Corps and graduate from "boot camp." Our motivation in each case was probably very different and was generated from a different source. The decision to join the Marine Corps was more than likely based upon the desire to serve the United States or the need to prove ourselves. This need or desire was probably fulfilled because of the desire to prove that we were Marine Corps material as well as the need to avoid the wrath of our Drill Instructor. These desires and needs were probably generated by both our Drill Instructor and within ourselves. In both cases, we had needs or desires that caused us to do certain things.

The leader must understand and ensure that his/her Marines understand that everything we do as Marines is designed to constantly sharpen our ability to succeed in battle. Every Marine must be committed to this goal. Motivation is the willingness of the individual to function as a part of the Marine team.

Motivation in advertising is the willingness of the individual to function as a part of the agency. The agency is there to make great creative work. The enemies to great creative work are about one thing and one thing only...timing.

Great work takes time.

A great agency has a killer account team that will fight for that time so the rest of the agency can do their work. While not every role is a creative role, just like not every role is not an infantry role, the agency serves the creative. The people in those agencies, no matter what department, are creative if you ask me. I feel like almost everyone in the ad business has some creative elements about their being. It's why finance teams will take jobs at agencies instead of wall street or the city. They could make twice as much but they'd be working in a corporate environment where everyone essentially wears a uniform. (Just follow the handle, @midtownuniform on IG and you'll see.)

If you want to keep wearing a uniform when you transition out of the military, then this book probably isn't for you. I did run into one reservist, an Air National Guardsman, while at Ogilvy. It's not like you can't do both, if the weekend warrior thing is your thing. You can. It's just I never went that route and I didn't go that route on purpose. I wanted to step back into the civilian population bringing the leadership principles I learned to the advertising industry and see where it got me. There is a trail to the top of every mountain but the view of the moon from the top is always the same.

After 10 years in advertising I landed in the Lower Hudson Valley with a beautiful family, and I love the view of the moon from our backyard.

Now, with my 5-year tenure 'swinging with the wing' in the Marines and my 10 years building brands with the top brands in the ad business, I am confident I can do just about anything. I made it here in New York, in large part, thanks to my motivation. It is one of the key contributors to my success in this business.

It's my opinion that motivation and enthusiasm are contagious, but there are ways to develop motivation that we find, again, in our handy manual on leadership from the Marines (MCTP 6-10B):

Developing motivation among Marines:
1. *Be motivated and enthusiastic.*
2. *Maintain positive relationships with his/her Marines.*
3. *Provide the basic needs all Marines share:*
    a. *Food, shelter and water.*
    b. *Social needs (i.e. comradeship).*
    c. *Protection from danger, threat and deprivation.*
    d. *Self-respect.*
4. *Ensure that each individual Marine fulfills his/her comrades' expectations, such as:*
    a. *Proficiency in his/her job.*
    b. *Self-discipline.*
    c. *Commitment and pride as a team member.*
5. *Provide tough, realistic unit training when possible.*
6. *Enhance a Marine's motivation to perform well; ensure he/she knows that he/she:*
    a. *Can succeed if they try hard enough.*
    b. *Will be recognized for good work.*
    c. *Will be punished for a lack of effort.*
    d. *Plays a critical role in determining the success or failure of the unit.*

What are some guidelines the leader can follow to obtain good performance from his/her Marines?
1. *Establish challenging, attainable goals within the capabilities of his/her Marines.*
2. *Create the assurance that good performance will be rewarded.*
3. *Strive to align personal goals with unit goals.*
4. *Recognize good work.*
5. *Take prompt action against poor performance.*

These are brass tacks, nuts and bolts, bare bones fundamentals if you want to keep anybody motivated. Marine or no Marine. Take these basics to your agency of choice anywhere in the world and crush it. Keep up your enthusiasm and motivation, no matter what you run into along the way. If you stay motivated and enthusiastic long enough, enough people around you will get motivated and enthusiastic, too. When you get that *esprit de corps* feeling at an agency and you're surrounded by creative people, the work gets real fun and the parties get even more fun.

Holiday parties are usually the best chance to take a reading on the *esprit de corps* of the agency. You don't get a jammin' holiday party just by serving top shelf booze and quality tapas. It takes a year or two of following these principles from the top down in order to get the kind of unit cohesion that really feels like something special.

Work at fostering *esprit de corps* by exemplifying the leadership principles yourself and it becomes contagious. It will spread to others like wildfire. I've been doing it for ten years and the motivation and enthusiasm has never failed me.

If you want your next holiday party to really resonate with the cosmos, let's have a quick look at how the Marines implement *esprit de corps* per our trusty manual (MCTP 6-10B):

How can a leader foster esprit de corps?

1. *The leader must embody the fighting spirit he/she wants to develop.*
2. *Indoctrinate new Marines by ensuring they are properly welcomed into the unit. Include an explanation of the unit's history, traditions and its present mission and activity.*
3. *Train your Marines as a team.*
4. *Develop the feeling that the unit as a whole must succeed.*
5. *Instruct them in history and traditions.*
6. *Leaders must use ingenuity and initiative to train their own minds, so that they can provide to their Marines useful and meaningful instruction.*
7. *Attain and maintain within the unit a high level of physical conditioning and proficiency in the military skills.*
8. *Recognize and publish the achievements of the unit and its members. Reinforce all positive performance.*
9. *Make use of appropriate and proper ceremonies, slogans, and symbols.*
10. *Use competition wisely to foster a team concept; try to win in every competition. Always find some way to convince others your unit is the best.*
11. *Employ your command in accordance with its capabilities in order to maximize its chances of success.*
12. *Make proper use of decorations and awards.*
13. *Make your Marines feel they are invincible, that the success of the Corps and country depends on them and the victory of their unit.*

Now I'm not trying to claim that someone like me, a humble Sergeant of Marines, and simple diesel engine mechanic (6072) for the Marine Aircraft Wing, knows best. I'm also not claiming that of all of the marketing and advertising professionals out there, I've got the best perspective, either. My perspective is my perspective. I'm one passenger here on this spaceship and if you've made it this far, then you might just listen to my perspective and my perception of the world:

> *A life lived in and adjacent to creativity is a life not wasted. I love my Marines. I love my veterans. I love what advertising has given me and I want to give back to both communities. I would like to see more Marines and veterans in advertising and marketing roles because I believe these communities will benefit from each other.*

That's all, dear motivator. If you're a Marine, a veteran, even an ROTC student, or just a plain old motivator in the industry looking to hone your leadership skills because you respect the military, thank you for reading my book. Thank you for passing it on to another motivator who might find it useful.

Lastly, if you want to get at me, you can find me on the web at brettgjones.com; and, on Twitter @bgjones. Godspeed.

Afterward - On Quantum Entanglement

Have you heard about that entangled motivation? That's my favorite kind. You're here, reading words I wrote. You're bonding through space-time using coded colors, divided just so into a fancy font, on a piece of the physicality that manifests through light energy bouncing around just right. The energy you're holding, whether you're reading it on your Kindle, in print, or on the Internet, is the direct result of the energy I stroked into the cosmos, key by key, straight from the synaptic connections lobbing light around my dome piece. This book ain't called *transformational* because Jones is just an 'ad guy,' dear motivator. He's a polycosmic systems buster, on call, ready to drive change in an industry that could use a dose of basic training in the fundamentals of leadership. Give this book to the next motivator you see with a creative drive and a warrior spirit.

Let our entangled motivation surf along this cosmic wave for as long as it may ride...

...semper fidelis, motivators.

Fig. 1: MCRD San Diego on July 1st, 2002: Private First Class, Brett G. Jones, USMC

Fig. 2: Hudson Farms on April 11th, 2018 (from left to right, and with permission):

1) General James T. Conway, USMC (Ret. 1970-2010), 34th Commandant of the Marine Corps;

2) Brett G. Jones, USMC (Vet. 2002-2007), Sergeant, 910 Division, MALS-16;

3) Lieutenant General John F. Sattler, USMC (Ret. 1971-2008) Director of Strategic Plans and Policy, U.S. Joint Chiefs of Staff

...motivate.